Fukushima Fallout: Unveiling the Truth behind the 2011 Nuclear Disaster

Oliver Lancaster

Published by Oliver Lancaster, 2023.

FUKUSHIMA FALLOUT: UNVEILING THE TRUTH BEHIND THE 2011 NUCLEAR DISASTER

First edition. July 2, 2023.

Copyright © 2023 Oliver Lancaster.

ISBN: 979-8215340097

Written by Oliver Lancaster.

Also by Oliver Lancaster

Chernobyl: Unveiling the tragedy. A Comprehensive Account of the Nuclear Disaster

The Bhopal Gas Tragedy: Unraveling the Catastrophe of 1984

The Deepwater Horizon Oil Spill of 2010: A Disaster Unveiled

Fukushima Fallout: Unveiling the Truth behind the 2011 Nuclear Disaster

Minamata Disease: Poisoned Waters and the Battle for Justice (1932-1968)

Watch for more at https://tinyurl.com/olanc.

Sign up to my free newsletter to get updates on new releases, FREE teaser chapters to upcoming releases and FREE digital short stories.

Or visit https://tinyurl.com/olanc

I never spam and you can unsubscribe at any time.

Disclaimer

The information presented in "Fukushima Fallout: Unveiling the Truth behind the 2011 Nuclear Disaster" is based on extensive research and available sources. While every effort has been made to ensure accuracy, it is important to note that the field of nuclear energy and the Fukushima disaster continue to evolve. New developments, scientific findings, and revised perspectives may have emerged since the publication of this book. Readers are encouraged to consult up-to-date sources and expert opinions for the latest information on the Fukushima disaster and related topics. The author and publisher disclaim any liability for any loss or damage incurred by readers relying on the information provided in this book.

OLIVER LANCASTER

Fukushima Fallout: Unveiling the Truth behind the 2011 Nuclear Disaster

FUKUSHIMA FALLOUT: UNVEILING THE TRUTH BEHIND THE 2011 NUCLEAR DISASTER

FUKUSHIMA FALLOUT: UNVEILING THE TRUTH BEHIND THE 2011 NUCLEAR DISASTER

Introduction: The Birth of Fukushima Daiichi: A Historical Overview

The Construction and Design of the Fukushima Daiichi Nuclear Power Plant

The Fukushima Daiichi Nuclear Power Plant, often regarded as a symbol of the grave nuclear disaster that struck Japan in 2011, traces its origins back to a time when nuclear energy held the promise of a better future. Its construction was heralded as a significant step towards embracing a new era of power generation, fostering Japan's rapid economic development.

The plant, located in the towns of Okuma and Futaba in the Futaba District of Fukushima Prefecture, was built by the Tokyo Electric Power Company (TEPCO). Construction began in 1967, marking a new milestone in Japan's nuclear energy history. The Fukushima Daiichi plant was designed to be one of the largest nuclear power plants globally, reflecting Japan's ambitious goals in the sector.

The design of the Fukushima Daiichi Nuclear Power Plant was composed of six separate boiling water reactors (BWRs), a type of light water nuclear reactor. General Electric (GE) supplied the first three units, units 1, 2, and 3. Toshiba provided units 3 and 5, while Hitachi was responsible for unit 4. Each unit was built and came online in stages between 1971 and 1979, supplying a total electrical power capacity of approximately 4.7 GW.

The plant's design incorporated several safety features, reflecting the industry's understanding of nuclear safety at the time. The reactor cores were housed within primary containment vessels designed to prevent the release of radioactive materials in the event of an accident. These primary containment vessels were enclosed within secondary containment structures, or reactor buildings, designed to protect against both external threats and potential internal mishaps.

One of the most critical safety features was the emergency cooling system. In case of a loss of coolant accident (LOCA), the system was designed to automatically inject water into the reactor core to prevent overheating and a potential meltdown. In addition, a backup diesel generator system was in place to provide power to the cooling system in case of a complete station blackout.

However, some aspects of the plant's design and location were later criticized following the 2011 disaster. For instance, the Fukushima Daiichi plant was built close to the sea level—only 10 meters above sea level. While this facilitated the access to sea water for cooling purposes, it also made the plant susceptible to tsunamis, a risk underscored by the plant's location on the Pacific Ring of Fire, a region known for its seismic activity.

The design also relied on active safety systems, such as diesel generators and cooling systems that required a power source to operate. This reliance on active systems would later prove to be a significant weakness when the plant was hit by the earthquake and subsequent tsunami that led to a station blackout.

The Fukushima Daiichi Nuclear Power Plant, once the embodiment of Japan's nuclear aspirations, was a complex interplay of advanced design, ambitious goals, and inherent risks. While it was built with the safety standards of its time, the disaster in 2011 underscored that these measures were not sufficient to withstand the extreme natural forces it eventually faced. In retrospect, the construction and design of the Fukushima Daiichi plant provide crucial insights into the challenges and potential pitfalls of nuclear power generation.

Japan's Reliance on Nuclear Power and Energy Policies

JAPAN'S RELIANCE ON nuclear power has been a complex issue, underscored by the country's unique energy landscape. As a resource-poor nation, Japan has limited domestic energy sources, which has shaped its energy policies since the early post-war era. Nuclear power, viewed as a home-grown and stable energy supply, played a pivotal role in Japan's energy mix.

In the 1970s, the oil crisis severely impacted Japan's economy, which was heavily dependent on imported oil. This crisis triggered a strategic shift in Japan's energy policy towards diversification of energy sources, promoting nuclear energy as a viable and more independent alternative. By the end of the 20th century, Japan had established itself as one of the world's leading nuclear power users.

The government's Basic Energy Plan, first established in 2003 and revised every three years, set ambitious targets for nuclear energy. The 2010 plan, the year before the Fukushima disaster, aimed to increase the country's nuclear energy supply to over 50% by 2030, underscoring the country's deep reliance on this power source.

However, the 2011 Fukushima Daiichi nuclear disaster was a turning point in Japan's nuclear power policy. The severe accident and subsequent fallout exposed the vulnerabilities in Japan's nuclear energy policy, leading to nationwide introspection and policy review. The disaster raised significant public concerns about the safety of nuclear power plants, prompting the shutdown of most of the country's nuclear reactors for safety inspections and upgrades.

In the aftermath of the disaster, Japan's energy policy underwent a significant shift. The country was forced to increase its reliance on imported fossil fuels to compensate for the loss of nuclear power, leading to an increase in energy prices and greenhouse gas emissions. Simultaneously, there was a concerted effort to increase investment in renewable energy, energy conservation, and efficiency measures.

Japan's Strategic Energy Plan of 2014 laid out a new approach to energy policy. It aimed for a diverse energy supply-and-demand structure, reducing dependency on nuclear power, and promoting renewables. However, the plan still considers nuclear energy as an essential base-load power source, suggesting that Japan has not completely moved away from its reliance on nuclear power.

The balance between nuclear and other energy sources remains a contentious issue in Japan. While there is a growing public sentiment towards a transition to a more sustainable and safer energy mix, concerns about energy security, economic efficiency, and climate change mitigation make it challenging to phase out nuclear power entirely.

Japan is still grappling with these issues. The government's plans for the future energy mix, as well as the long-term fate of its nuclear power plants, including the decommissioned Fukushima Daiichi plant, are subjects of ongoing debate, reflecting the complexity of the country's energy landscape.

Chapter 1: The Great East Japan Earthquake: Unleashing the Disaster

The Earthquake and Tsunami that Struck Japan on March 11, 2011

The event that would forever redefine Japan's relationship with nuclear power and spark a global conversation about the safety of nuclear energy occurred on March 11, 2011. On this fateful day, Japan was hit by one of the most powerful earthquakes in recorded history, triggering a devastating tsunami that would escalate into the Fukushima Daiichi nuclear disaster.

The earthquake, known as the Great East Japan Earthquake (Tohoku earthquake), struck at 2:46 pm local time. The epicenter was located off the northeastern coast of the Japanese mainland, the Tōhoku region, approximately 70 kilometers east of the Oshika Peninsula of Miyagi Prefecture. The quake was exceptionally powerful, with a magnitude of 9.0 to 9.1 on the Richter scale, making it the most potent earthquake ever to hit Japan and the fourth most powerful in the world since modern record-keeping began in the early 20th century.

The tremors were felt widely across the region, causing widespread destruction and loss of life. However, it was the subsequent tsunami that unleashed the most significant devastation. Generated by the enormous displacement of water due to the undersea earthquake, the tsunami waves reached heights of up to 40 meters in some areas, travelling at high speeds towards the eastern coast of Japan.

Within an hour of the earthquake, the first tsunami waves hit the shoreline, ravaging coastal communities. The powerful waves overran sea walls and flooded cities and towns, sweeping away buildings, cars, and anything else in their path. The impact of the tsunami was catastrophic, causing extensive loss of life and property.

One of the most heavily impacted sites was the Fukushima Daiichi Nuclear Power Plant. The plant's design had accounted for earthquakes, and it initially withstood the seismic event. When the earthquake struck, the operating reactors - Units 1, 2, and 3 - automatically shut down, as per design. However, the incoming tsunami far exceeded the design parameters. The plant, built only 10 meters above sea level, was unprepared for the approximately 15-meter tsunami wave that swept over its sea wall.

The tsunami inundated the power plant, knocking out the backup diesel generators designed to provide power for the plant's cooling systems in an emergency. This led to a loss of power, triggering a series of events that culminated in a severe nuclear crisis: the Fukushima Daiichi nuclear disaster.

The earthquake and tsunami of March 11, 2011, were natural disasters of an almost unimaginable scale. Their direct impact was devastating, causing a humanitarian crisis that Japan is still grappling with. However, the ensuing nuclear disaster at the

Fukushima Daiichi plant added another layer of complexity to the tragedy, sparking a serious reevaluation of nuclear safety and policy both in Japan and worldwide.

Initial Impact on the Fukushima Daiichi Nuclear Power Plant

THE FUKUSHIMA DAIICHI Nuclear Power Plant faced a cascading series of failures following the Great East Japan Earthquake and subsequent tsunami on March 11, 2011. Despite initial resilience to the earthquake, the plant was critically vulnerable to the enormous tsunami wave that swiftly followed.

When the 9.0 magnitude earthquake struck, the three operational reactors at the time—Units 1, 2, and 3—automatically tripped, causing them to shut down immediately, a safety feature known as a scram. This shutdown halted the nuclear fission process, but it did not completely stop the production of heat. A significant amount of residual heat, also called decay heat, continued to be produced due to the radioactive decay of fission products within the reactor core.

To remove this decay heat and prevent the reactor core from overheating, the reactor's cooling system needs to function correctly. Under normal circumstances, this is powered by the electricity grid. However, the earthquake damaged the external power supply to the Fukushima Daiichi plant. To counter this, emergency diesel generators, a component of the plant's safety system, were designed to kick in when the primary power source was lost.

Initially, the system worked as intended. The diesel generators started and took over the critical role of powering the cooling systems. However, the ensuing tsunami, with waves reaching up to 15 meters, far surpassed the plant's defensive design parameters and struck approximately 50 minutes after the earthquake.

The tsunami inundated the plant, flooding the buildings that housed the emergency diesel generators and the electrical switchgear. This resulted in the loss of backup power, a scenario known as a station blackout (SBO). Without power, the cooling systems failed, and the situation at the Fukushima Daiichi plant quickly became critical.

Without proper cooling, the fuel rods' temperature in the reactor cores of Units 1, 2, and 3 began to rise rapidly. The high temperatures caused a reaction between the fuel rod claddings and the steam, producing hydrogen gas—a development that would later lead to severe explosions.

In the direct aftermath of the tsunami, TEPCO and the plant workers scrambled to manage the crisis. They initiated measures to vent pressure from the containment vessels and started the process of injecting seawater into the reactors to cool them down, marking the start of a long and challenging battle to regain control of the reactors.

The initial impact of the earthquake and tsunami set the stage for one of the most severe nuclear disasters in history. It underlined the vulnerability of even the most robust systems in the face of extreme natural forces and raised questions about the adequacy of existing safety measures and regulations in nuclear power plants worldwide.

Chapter 2: Understanding Nuclear Reactors and Meltdown

Basics of Nuclear Reactors and Their Operation

A nuclear reactor is a complex system designed to sustain a nuclear chain reaction and control it safely. It harnesses the energy produced by nuclear fission to generate electricity. The following provides a basic overview of how nuclear reactors operate.

At the core of a nuclear reactor are fuel rods, which contain pellets of fissionable material, typically uranium-235 or plutonium-239. When a neutron strikes the nucleus of one of these atoms, it can cause the nucleus to split, or undergo fission. This fission process releases a significant amount of energy in the form of heat and radiation, along with more neutrons, which can then trigger further fission reactions, creating a chain reaction.

A vital part of a nuclear reactor's operation is controlling this chain reaction. This is achieved through control rods, made from materials that absorb neutrons, such as boron or cadmium. By inserting or removing these control rods from the reactor core, operators can regulate the rate of the fission chain reaction. If the control rods are fully inserted into the core, they absorb a large number of neutrons, effectively halting the chain reaction. Conversely, withdrawing the control rods allows more neutrons to cause fission, increasing the reaction rate.

The heat generated from the fission process is used to produce steam. In a boiling water reactor (BWR), like those at Fukushima Daiichi, the reactor coolant—water—is boiled directly in the reactor core. The produced steam drives a turbine connected to an electricity generator.

Once the steam passes through the turbine, it is condensed back into water in a condenser and then returned to the reactor core, completing the loop. This method allows for the efficient use of heat energy produced from the nuclear reactions.

However, one critical aspect of a nuclear reactor is the need for continuous cooling, even after the fission process is stopped. When a reactor is shut down, it still produces a significant amount of residual heat from the radioactive decay of fission products. This "decay heat" needs to be removed to prevent the reactor core from overheating, which can lead to a meltdown—a catastrophic event where the nuclear fuel becomes so hot that it forms a molten mass, potentially releasing large amounts of radioactive material.

Several safety systems are in place to provide cooling in the event of abnormal conditions or accidents. One of these is the emergency core cooling system, designed to provide cooling if the regular cooling system fails. However, these systems are often dependent on an external power source to operate, making them vulnerable in a situation like a station blackout, which occurred at the Fukushima Daiichi Nuclear Power Plant.

The operation of a nuclear reactor thus involves a delicate balance between harnessing the power of nuclear fission to generate electricity and ensuring that this power is carefully controlled and cooled to prevent accidents.

The Causes and Consequences of a Reactor Meltdown

A REACTOR MELTDOWN is one of the most severe accidents that can occur in a nuclear power plant. It involves the catastrophic failure of the reactor core, leading to the melting of nuclear fuel elements, and potentially, the release of significant amounts of radioactive material. Understanding the causes and consequences of a reactor meltdown is crucial for grasping the magnitude of the Fukushima Daiichi disaster.

Causes

THE PRIMARY CAUSE OF a reactor meltdown is the loss of proper cooling to the reactor core. When a nuclear reactor operates, it generates a significant amount of heat due to the nuclear fission process. Even after the reactor is shut down, a substantial amount of residual heat continues to be produced due to the radioactive decay of fission products. If this heat is not adequately removed, it can lead to a rise in the reactor core's temperature, ultimately causing the fuel elements to melt - a condition referred to as a reactor meltdown.

Several scenarios can lead to the loss of cooling. One is a complete loss of power to the reactor site, also known as a station blackout, as happened at Fukushima. Without power, the reactor's cooling systems cannot operate. Another scenario could be a major breach in the reactor coolant system, leading to the loss of coolant. This type of incident is referred to as a loss-of-coolant accident (LOCA).

Consequences

THE CONSEQUENCES OF a reactor meltdown can be severe and far-reaching. Initially, the melting of the reactor core can lead to a buildup of pressure within the reactor containment structures due to the generation of steam and other gases. If not properly managed, this pressure buildup can lead to an explosion, which can further damage the reactor structures and potentially lead to the release of radioactive material.

One of the significant risks of a meltdown is the potential release of radioactive materials into the environment. If the containment structures are breached, radioactive isotopes can escape, contaminating the air, soil, and water. The release of these materials can have severe environmental and health effects, leading to an increase in the risk of cancer and other diseases among exposed populations. The cleanup and decontamination process following such a release can be time-consuming and costly.

A meltdown also results in the total loss of the reactor itself, requiring a complex and dangerous decommissioning process.

FUKUSHIMA FALLOUT: UNVEILING THE TRUTH BEHIND THE 2011 NUCLEAR DISASTER

The melted reactor core, often referred to as corium, is highly radioactive and challenging to manage and remove.

The reactor meltdown at the Fukushima Daiichi Nuclear Power Plant resulted in the release of radioactive materials, the displacement of local populations, and long-lasting environmental and health effects. It also significantly impacted Japan's energy policies and the global perspective on nuclear power, highlighting the critical importance of adequate safety measures in nuclear power plant design and operation.

Chapter 3: Chernobyl vs. Fukushima: A Comparison of Nuclear Disasters

---

Similarities and Differences Between the Chernobyl and Fukushima Disasters

The nuclear accidents at Chernobyl in 1986 and Fukushima Daiichi in 2011 represent two of the most severe nuclear disasters in history. Both events resulted in significant releases of radioactive materials, had substantial human and environmental impacts, and caused major disruptions to the energy policies of their respective countries. However, the causes, progression, and aftermath of the two incidents differed in several key ways.

Similarities

1. SEVERITY: Both the Chernobyl and Fukushima disasters are classified as level 7 events on the International Nuclear Event Scale (INES), the highest rating, indicating a "major accident" with "widespread health and environmental effects."

2. Evacuation and relocation: Both disasters necessitated the evacuation and long-term displacement of local populations due to high radiation levels. In each case, a large exclusion zone was established around the plant, within which habitation remains restricted even years after the incidents.

3. Long-term environmental and health impact: Both disasters resulted in the significant release of radioactive materials into the environment, causing long-lasting contamination of air, soil, and water. This contamination has led to increased risks of cancer and other health effects among exposed populations.

Differences

1. CAUSE AND PROGRESSION of the accident: The causes of the two disasters were fundamentally different. The Chernobyl accident was primarily a result of a flawed reactor design and serious mistakes made by the plant operators during a safety test. In contrast, the Fukushima Daiichi disaster was triggered by a massive natural disaster – a powerful earthquake followed by a tsunami – that led to a station blackout, disabling the cooling systems of the reactors.

2. Containment and release of radioactivity: The containment structures at Fukushima largely fulfilled their function, despite the severity of the accident. The majority of the radioactive materials remained within the reactor buildings, and the released materials were largely due to venting operations and hydrogen explosions. In contrast, at Chernobyl, the reactor lacked a proper containment structure. The initial steam explosion and subsequent graphite fire led to a substantial release of radioactive materials directly into the atmosphere.

3. Immediate human casualties: The Chernobyl disaster resulted in the immediate death of 31 people due to the explosion and acute radiation sickness. At Fukushima, there were no immediate radiation-related deaths. The fatalities were due to the natural disaster and the subsequent evacuation process.

4. Technological factors: The reactors involved in the accidents were of different designs. Chernobyl's Reactor 4 was a high-power channel-type reactor (RBMK), a design unique to the Soviet Union, with known safety issues. Fukushima's reactors were boiling water reactors (BWRs), a widely used and generally well-regarded design, albeit with vulnerabilities exposed by the disaster.

While both the Chernobyl and Fukushima Daiichi disasters are remembered as two of the most catastrophic nuclear accidents, they represent different types of accidents with unique causes, sequences of events, and long-term implications. These two incidents serve as stark reminders of the potential risks associated with nuclear power and the need for stringent safety measures and robust disaster management plans.

Lessons Learned from Chernobyl and Their Application to Fukushima

THE NUCLEAR DISASTERS at Chernobyl in 1986 and Fukushima Daiichi in 2011 underscored the potential hazards of nuclear power and reshaped our understanding of nuclear safety. The lessons learned from these accidents have been instrumental in reforming nuclear safety protocols and emergency response measures globally. However, as the

Fukushima Daiichi accident demonstrated, applying these lessons effectively presents its own set of challenges.

Lessons from Chernobyl

ONE OF THE CRITICAL lessons from the Chernobyl disaster was the importance of reactor design. The reactor at Chernobyl was an RBMK type, which had significant design flaws, such as a positive void coefficient, making it inherently unstable under certain conditions. This realization led to a renewed focus on the safety aspects of reactor design, including intrinsic safety features and multiple, independent, and redundant safety systems.

The Chernobyl accident also highlighted the necessity of a strong and independent regulatory body to oversee nuclear power operations. Prior to the accident, the Soviet nuclear industry lacked sufficient regulatory oversight, which contributed to lax safety culture and procedures. In response to this, many countries strengthened their nuclear regulatory bodies and emphasized their independence from the industries they regulate.

Chernobyl underscored the importance of clear and timely communication during a nuclear crisis. The initial Soviet response was marked by secrecy and misinformation, which exacerbated the disaster's effects and hampered international assistance efforts. This lesson led to improvements in international cooperation, transparency protocols, and crisis communication during nuclear emergencies.

Application to Fukushima

THE LESSONS FROM CHERNOBYL influenced many aspects of the nuclear industry's approach to safety, and some of these lessons were reflected in the response to the Fukushima Daiichi disaster. However, the Fukushima accident also exposed areas where the application of these lessons had fallen short.

In terms of reactor design, the Fukushima Daiichi plant's boiling water reactors were generally considered safer and more stable than the RBMK design used at Chernobyl. However, the Fukushima accident exposed design vulnerabilities in terms of location and defense against natural disasters—specifically, the plant's inadequate protection against tsunamis.

While Japan had a nuclear regulatory body in place at the time of the Fukushima disaster, subsequent investigations revealed that it had significant ties to the nuclear industry and had often prioritized the promotion of nuclear power over stringent safety oversight. This situation, reminiscent of the pre-Chernobyl era, led to criticism of Japan's nuclear regulation and calls for it to be made more robust and independent.

In terms of crisis communication, Japan was more transparent and forthcoming than the Soviet Union had been during Chernobyl. However, there were still issues with timeliness, clarity, and coordination of communication, which led to public confusion and mistrust.

While the lessons from Chernobyl did lead to significant improvements in the safety and regulation of nuclear power, the Fukushima Daiichi disaster highlighted gaps in their implementation. It underscored the need for continuous learning, regular safety reassessments, and the importance of preparing for the unexpected in the realm of nuclear safety.

FUKUSHIMA FALLOUT: UNVEILING THE TRUTH BEHIND THE 2011 NUCLEAR DISASTER

Chapter 4: Emergency Response and Containment Efforts

Immediate Actions Taken to Prevent Further Damage

Following the earthquake and tsunami on March 11, 2011, the situation at the Fukushima Daiichi Nuclear Power Plant quickly escalated. Faced with a station blackout and a rapidly deteriorating condition in the reactors, the plant operators, TEPCO, and the Japanese government had to take swift actions to prevent further damage and the possible release of significant amounts of radioactive materials.

1. Injection of cooling water: As the temperatures in the reactor cores of Units 1, 2, and 3 began to rise following the loss of cooling, one of the immediate actions taken was to inject cooling water into the reactors. Initially, fresh water was used, but as the situation continued to deteriorate and supplies ran low, seawater was used. This step was crucial in preventing the complete meltdown of the reactor cores and a potentially even larger release of radioactive materials.

2. Venting of reactor containment vessels: The rising temperature and pressure inside the reactor containment vessels created the risk of their rupture, which would have led to a significant release of radioactivity. To prevent this, venting operations were conducted. This involved releasing some of the gases inside the containment vessels to reduce the pressure. While this action did lead to the release of some radioactive materials, it was deemed necessary to prevent a more catastrophic failure of the containment structures.

3. Evacuation and establishment of exclusion zones: In the wake of the accident, the Japanese government declared an atomic energy disaster situation and initiated evacuation orders. Initially, a 3 km radius around the plant was designated as an exclusion zone, but this was soon expanded to 20 km as the severity of the situation became clearer. These steps were taken to protect the public from potential radiation exposure.

4. International assistance: Given the severity of the situation, international assistance was sought. The U.S. Navy provided water cannons to help with the cooling efforts. Additionally, TEPCO and the Japanese government worked with the International Atomic Energy Agency (IAEA) and nuclear experts worldwide to manage the crisis.

5. Stabilization of spent fuel pools: The spent fuel pools, particularly in Unit 4, also posed a significant risk. Without adequate cooling, the water in these pools could have evaporated, exposing the spent fuel rods, which could have led to a significant release of radiation. Water was sprayed into these pools to keep them filled and the spent fuel rods covered.

These immediate actions helped stabilize the situation at the Fukushima Daiichi plant and played a significant role in mitigating the scale of the disaster. The efforts of the plant workers, often referred to as the "Fukushima 50," were crucial during this phase. They worked under extremely difficult and dangerous conditions to execute these countermeasures, often putting their lives at risk in the process.

The immediate response to the Fukushima disaster provided several important lessons for managing nuclear emergencies, particularly regarding the importance of effective crisis communication, robust emergency protocols, and international cooperation.

Challenges Faced by Workers and Emergency Response Teams

THE FUKUSHIMA DAIICHI disaster presented a multitude of challenges for the workers on the ground and the emergency response teams. Faced with a complex and rapidly evolving crisis, these individuals had to navigate a series of obstacles while working under intense pressure and often dangerous conditions.

1. Extreme Working Conditions: The conditions on-site were extremely challenging. High levels of radiation, physical debris, and damage from the earthquake and tsunami, combined with frequent aftershocks, created a hazardous working environment. Despite these conditions, the plant workers—often referred to as the "Fukushima 50"—and emergency response teams worked tirelessly to mitigate the crisis.

2. High Radiation Levels: The increased radiation levels on-site posed a significant risk to workers' health, limiting the amount of time they could spend in certain areas of the plant. Special protective gear was required, which made the physical work even more challenging. Managing worker exposure to ensure it remained within safe limits was a constant challenge.

3. Communication Challenges: The loss of power and damage to infrastructure made communication difficult, both within the plant and with external entities. Providing accurate and timely information to decision-makers, the public, and international bodies like the IAEA was a constant challenge, given the rapidly evolving situation and the complex nature of the disaster.

4. Technical Challenges: The technical challenges faced by the workers and response teams were enormous. From injecting water into the reactors, venting the reactor containment vessels, managing spent fuel pools, to eventually laying the groundwork for a "cold shutdown," each task required careful planning, expertise, and often improvisation given the unprecedented nature of the crisis.

5. Psychological Stress: The immense psychological stress cannot be overlooked. Many workers were local residents, with families directly impacted by the earthquake, tsunami, and nuclear disaster. The uncertainty, combined with the enormous responsibility and dangerous working conditions, put a considerable psychological burden on the workers.

6. Limited Resources and Manpower: The plant's remote location, combined with the broader impact of the earthquake and tsunami on the region, meant resources and manpower were stretched thin. Assistance had to be coordinated from other parts of Japan and internationally, which presented logistical challenges.

Despite these challenges, the workers and emergency response teams at Fukushima showed immense courage and resilience. Their efforts played a crucial role in preventing an even greater disaster and underlined the human aspect of the crisis. Their experiences have provided valuable lessons for emergency preparedness and response in the context of nuclear accidents.

38

Chapter 5: Radioactive Releases: Assessing the Environmental Impact

Measuring the Extent of Radioactive Contamination

Determining the extent of radioactive contamination following a nuclear disaster like Fukushima Daiichi involves complex scientific procedures and careful data analysis. It is essential for understanding the impact on the environment and human health, guiding cleanup efforts, and establishing when and where it is safe for displaced residents to return.

Several different types of measurements and techniques are used to evaluate radioactive contamination.

1. Airborne Monitoring: After the disaster, airborne radiation monitoring was carried out to measure the radioactive materials released into the atmosphere. This included using aircraft equipped with radiation detectors to provide a broad overview of the contamination spread, as well as ground-based air sampling for more localized data.

2. Soil Sampling: Soil samples were collected from across a wide area and analyzed to determine the types and levels of radioactive isotopes present. This provided crucial information on the ground contamination, which affects agriculture and determines whether it is safe for people to live in the area.

3. Water Monitoring: Both seawater and freshwater sources were monitored for radioactive contamination. This included sampling and analyzing water from the ocean, rivers, reservoirs, and groundwater sources. In the case of Fukushima, where large amounts of contaminated water were discharged into the ocean, this was a critical aspect of the monitoring effort.

4. Food and Agricultural Testing: Contamination can enter the food chain through crops, livestock, and seafood, posing a risk to human health. Rigorous testing of food products was carried out to ensure food safety and establish restrictions on the distribution and consumption of food from affected areas.

5. Dosimetry: This involves measuring the radiation dose that individuals have received. For workers involved in the emergency response and cleanup, personal dosimeters were used. In the wider population, measurements were taken to assess external radiation levels, and in some cases, whole-body counters were used to measure internal radiation levels.

6. Radiation Mapping: All of this data was used to create detailed maps of the radiation levels in different areas. This was vital for decision-making processes around evacuation and relocation, ongoing monitoring of the situation, and planning decontamination efforts.

These measurements and their analysis presented significant challenges, given the scale of the disaster and the need for rapid, accurate data. Despite these difficulties, the data collected in the aftermath of the Fukushima disaster represents an invaluable resource for understanding the behavior and impacts of radioactive contamination, informing future response strategies to nuclear incidents.

Effects on the Surrounding Environment, Wildlife, and Marine Life

THE RELEASE OF RADIOACTIVE materials from the Fukushima Daiichi disaster had wide-ranging effects on the environment, including land, forests, freshwater systems, and the ocean. The radioactive isotopes of most concern were iodine-131, cesium-134, and cesium-137, due to their relatively long half-lives and their potential to bioaccumulate in organisms and contaminate food chains.

Land and Forests

RADIOACTIVE MATERIALS from the plant were carried by wind and rain, contaminating a broad swathe of land, particularly to the northwest of the plant. Forests in these areas were particularly affected as the removal of radioactive contaminants from forest ecosystems is challenging, leading to persistent contamination. There's concern about the re-suspension and runoff of these radioactive materials, potentially re-contaminating decontaminated areas and infiltrating freshwater systems.

Freshwater Systems

FRESHWATER SYSTEMS, including rivers and lakes, showed elevated levels of radioactive cesium following the disaster. This contamination posed risks to freshwater species and potentially humans, through the consumption of contaminated freshwater fish and shellfish. Over time, the radioactive levels in these systems have gradually decreased due to the decay of the isotopes and the actions of water and sediments, which can dilute and sequester the contaminants.

Ocean and Marine Life

THE FUKUSHIMA DAIICHI disaster resulted in the most extensive release of radioactive material into the ocean in history. This was due to both the initial disaster and the subsequent controlled releases of contaminated water used for cooling the reactors. Radioactive isotopes were detected in seawater and marine sediments near the plant, with levels decreasing with distance from the plant.

Marine life also showed signs of contamination, particularly bottom-dwelling fish near the Fukushima coast, and some species of fish and shellfish exceeded the Japanese regulatory limits for human consumption. Over time, the levels of radioactivity in most marine species have declined, reflecting the decreased concentration in seawater and the ability of many marine organisms to eliminate cesium from their bodies.

Wildlife

DESPITE THE HIGH LEVELS of radiation in the affected areas, wildlife has shown resilience. Studies conducted in the years following the disaster found that many wildlife populations, including wild boar, Japanese macaques, and several bird species, have been able to persist in the contaminated zones. However, research also indicates potential radiation-induced changes in some species, such as decreased fertility and genetic mutations.

It's important to note that while the effects of radiation on individual organisms can be harmful, the impact on population levels is less clear, with many factors at play. Also, the apparent thriving of wildlife in the exclusion zone may be due to the absence of humans, rather than an indication that radiation is not harmful to these animals.

The long-term ecological consequences of the Fukushima Daiichi disaster are still being studied. It provides a somber reminder of the potential environmental impacts of nuclear accidents, informing guidelines for radiation protection for the environment, and shaping policies on nuclear safety and disaster response.

OLIVER LANCASTER

Chapter 6: Health Implications and Public Safety Concerns

Effects of Radiation Exposure on Human Health

The effects of radiation on human health depend on several factors, including the type and amount of radiation exposure, the duration of exposure, and the part of the body exposed. High levels of radiation exposure can have immediate effects, while long-term health impacts may emerge years after the exposure.

Acute Radiation Sickness: Acute radiation sickness, also known as radiation syndrome, occurs when an individual is exposed to a high dose of radiation over a short period. Symptoms can range from nausea, vomiting, and diarrhea to skin burns, changes in blood cell counts, and, in extreme cases, neurological problems and death. Fortunately, in the Fukushima Daiichi disaster, no workers or members of the public experienced radiation doses high enough to cause acute radiation sickness.

Cancer: Exposure to ionizing radiation increases the risk of developing cancer later in life. The radioactive isotopes of greatest concern in this respect are iodine-131 and cesium-137. Iodine-131, with its short half-life of eight days, is rapidly absorbed by the thyroid gland, particularly in children, and can increase the risk of thyroid cancer. Cesium-137, with its longer half-life of approximately 30 years, can expose people to radiation for a more extended period and increase the risk of various cancers.

Following the Fukushima disaster, comprehensive health checks, including thyroid ultrasound examinations, were conducted on all residents aged 18 or younger in Fukushima prefecture. As of my knowledge cutoff in 2021, while a number of thyroid cancers have been detected through these screenings, a clear link to radiation exposure from the disaster has not been established, with the observed rates potentially being due to the intensive screening process rather than an actual increase in incidence.

Mental Health: The mental health impacts of nuclear disasters are often significant and long-lasting. The stress and trauma associated with evacuation, displacement, and fear of radiation can lead to a range of mental health issues, including post-traumatic stress disorder (PTSD), depression, and anxiety. The stigma associated with being a nuclear disaster evacuee can also exacerbate these problems. Following the Fukushima disaster, increased rates of such mental health issues were observed among evacuees and others affected by the disaster.

Other Health Effects: Radiation can also have other health effects, including cardiovascular disease and cataracts, though the risk is generally less well understood than for cancer and typically requires higher doses of radiation.

It's important to note that the health effects of radiation exposure are subject to ongoing research. Continued health monitoring of those exposed to radiation from the Fukushima disaster, as well as further scientific studies, will provide a clearer understanding of the health impacts of such nuclear incidents.

Evacuation Efforts, Health Screenings, and Long-Term Consequences

IN THE AFTERMATH OF the Fukushima Daiichi nuclear disaster, large-scale evacuation efforts were implemented, extensive health screenings were conducted, and long-term consequences are still being evaluated and managed.

Evacuation Efforts

IN THE IMMEDIATE AFTERMATH of the disaster, the Japanese government established an evacuation zone around the Fukushima Daiichi plant. Initially set at a 3-kilometer radius, this was expanded to 20 kilometers as the severity of the nuclear crisis became apparent. Over 160,000 residents were evacuated from these zones, and many more chose to leave voluntarily from areas outside the official evacuation zone due to fear of radiation.

The evacuation process was fraught with challenges. Lack of communication and confusion over the severity of the crisis led to fear and panic among some residents. As is often the case in large-scale evacuations, vulnerable groups, including the elderly and those with disabilities or health issues, faced particular difficulties. Sadly, the stress and hardship of the evacuation contributed to what are termed "disaster-related deaths."

Health Screenings

IN THE WAKE OF THE nuclear disaster, extensive health checks were carried out on residents of Fukushima prefecture, particularly focusing on children and those who were in the area at the time of the disaster. These health checks included basic physical health screenings and mental health checkups.

One key aspect of the health screenings was the thyroid ultrasound examinations conducted on all residents aged 18 or younger. These screenings were due to the concern over radioactive iodine, which can increase the risk of thyroid cancer, particularly in children. The screenings led to the early detection of several cases of thyroid cancer, although whether these cases are directly linked to the nuclear disaster remains a subject of ongoing research and debate.

Long-Term Consequences

THE LONG-TERM CONSEQUENCES of the Fukushima Daiichi disaster are broad and complex. On the health front, continued monitoring and health care provision for those affected by the disaster is critical. This includes not only potential radiation-related health effects but also mental health issues associated with the trauma of the disaster and its aftermath.

In terms of social impacts, the disaster has led to long-term displacement for many residents. While some areas have been decontaminated and evacuation orders lifted, many former residents have chosen not to return due to ongoing concerns about radiation, lack of infrastructure and services, and the desire to move on with their lives in their new locations.

The disaster also had significant economic impacts, both in terms of the direct costs associated with the disaster response, compensation payments, and decontamination efforts, and the broader impact on the local and national economy.

Lastly, the Fukushima disaster had profound implications for Japan's energy policy, leading to a nationwide shutdown of nuclear power plants and a reevaluation of Japan's energy mix and future energy strategy.

The Fukushima Daiichi nuclear disaster has had far-reaching and long-lasting consequences, the full extent of which are still being understood and will be felt for decades to come.

OLIVER LANCASTER

Chapter 7: Media Coverage and Public Perception

International Media Coverage and Public Reaction to the Disaster

The Fukushima Daiichi nuclear disaster unfolded on the world stage, garnering extensive media coverage and eliciting a wide range of public reactions. The global scope of the disaster, combined with its multifaceted impacts, made it a significant event in international news and public discourse.

Media Coverage

INTERNATIONAL MEDIA provided extensive coverage of the disaster from the moment the earthquake and tsunami struck Japan on March 11, 2011. As the nuclear crisis at Fukushima Daiichi developed, the focus of the coverage increasingly shifted towards the unfolding nuclear disaster.

The media coverage played a vital role in disseminating information about the disaster, its causes, and its immediate and potential long-term effects. However, the reporting was not without its challenges. The rapidly evolving and highly complex nature of the nuclear crisis, coupled with initial underestimations and later revisions of the severity of the disaster, led to some confusion and misinformation. Some outlets were criticized for sensationalizing the nuclear aspect of the disaster, stoking fear and misunderstanding about radiation risks.

The disaster also raised questions about the role of the media in reporting on such complex and nuanced issues, highlighting the importance of accurate, balanced, and contextual reporting in the face of a crisis. The event led to increased efforts towards improving scientific literacy among journalists and promoting better communication between scientists, policymakers, and the media.

Public Reaction

THE PUBLIC REACTION to the Fukushima Daiichi disaster was one of shock and concern, both for the immediate humanitarian crisis caused by the earthquake and tsunami and for the unfolding nuclear disaster. The disaster occurred in a highly connected, digital age, allowing people worldwide to follow the event and its aftermath in real time.

In many countries, the disaster sparked public debates about the use of nuclear energy. Concerns about the safety of nuclear power plants, especially those located in seismic zones or coastal areas, were heightened. In some countries, this led to mass protests calling for a shift away from nuclear power.

Notably, in Germany, the public reaction to the Fukushima disaster was instrumental in shaping the government's decision to phase out all of its nuclear power plants. Switzerland and Belgium also made similar decisions, while other countries like France and the U.S. continued their commitment to nuclear energy, albeit with increased focus on safety.

The disaster also prompted many people to learn more about nuclear energy, radiation, and disaster preparedness, driving a surge of interest in these topics in the public sphere. It underscored the need for effective communication about nuclear energy and radiation risks to the public, to enable informed discussion and decision-making.

The international media coverage and public reaction to the Fukushima Daiichi disaster were integral parts of the event's global impact, influencing nuclear policies, public attitudes, and the discourse around nuclear energy and disaster preparedness.

The Role of Media in Disseminating Information and Shaping Public Opinion

THE MEDIA PLAYS A CRITICAL role in our society, particularly during times of crisis such as the Fukushima Daiichi nuclear disaster. As a primary source of information for the public, the media's role in disseminating information and shaping public opinion cannot be understated.

Disseminating Information

DURING THE FUKUSHIMA disaster, international media outlets were key in providing up-to-the-minute information about the unfolding crisis. With journalists stationed in Japan and experts providing analysis from around the world, media coverage played an essential role in keeping the public informed about the situation at the Fukushima Daiichi plant, the efforts to control it, and its impacts.

However, accurately reporting on a nuclear disaster is challenging. Nuclear science is complex and often misunderstood, and the situation at Fukushima was rapidly evolving and shrouded in uncertainty. While some media outlets provided accurate, nuanced coverage, others were criticized for oversimplifying, misrepresenting, or sensationalizing the information.

Moreover, in the early stages of the disaster, there was a lack of transparency and inconsistency in the information provided by the Japanese authorities and TEPCO. This created challenges for the media in reporting the situation accurately and contributed to public confusion and anxiety.

Shaping Public Opinion

MEDIA COVERAGE NOT only provides information but also plays a significant role in shaping public opinion. The way in which information is presented - the language used, the perspectives highlighted, the images shown - can significantly influence how the public perceives an event.

In the case of Fukushima, media coverage contributed to a heightened sense of fear and mistrust among some segments of the public. Graphic images of the damaged reactors and the use of phrases like "nuclear meltdown" invoked fear and invoked memories of past nuclear disasters like Chernobyl. At the same time, the lack of clear and consistent information from authorities fueled public mistrust and anxiety.

However, the media also played a positive role in driving public engagement and dialogue about nuclear energy. The coverage prompted many people to learn more about nuclear power, radiation, and disaster preparedness. It sparked public debates about the use of nuclear energy and influenced nuclear policies in several countries.

The Fukushima Daiichi disaster underscored the vital role of the media in a crisis and highlighted the challenges of reporting on complex scientific topics. It underscored the need for accurate, timely, and transparent communication, for fostering media literacy, and for involving scientists and experts in the communication process. It also demonstrated the profound influence of media on public opinion and policy-making.

OLIVER LANCASTER

Chapter 8: Government Response and Accountability

Analysis of the Japanese Government's Handling of the Crisis

The Japanese government's response to the Fukushima Daiichi nuclear disaster is a topic of extensive analysis and debate. The unprecedented nature of the disaster, coupled with its complex and rapidly evolving characteristics, presented immense challenges to the authorities.

Initial Response

IN THE IMMEDIATE AFTERMATH of the earthquake and tsunami, the government declared a state of emergency and started evacuating people living near the plant. These initial actions were crucial in ensuring that no lives were lost due to direct radiation exposure.

However, the government's early crisis communication faced criticism. The information released in the initial stages was often vague, inconsistent, or overly optimistic. This lack of transparency and apparent underestimation of the severity of the crisis led to confusion among the public and the international community, exacerbating fear and mistrust.

Evacuation and Health Checks

THE GOVERNMENT'S IMPLEMENTATION of evacuation orders, based on the progression of the nuclear disaster, was generally efficient. The creation of the exclusion zone and the orderly evacuation of residents undoubtedly helped prevent acute radiation sickness.

In the years following the disaster, the government organized extensive health checks for Fukushima residents, particularly children. These screenings allowed for monitoring of potential health effects and provided essential data for understanding the impact of the disaster on human health.

Decontamination Efforts and Support for Displaced Residents

THE GOVERNMENT HAS invested significantly in decontamination efforts, aiming to reduce radiation levels and make it possible for evacuees to return home. While these efforts have been successful in some areas, they have also faced criticism. The practicality and effectiveness of decontaminating large forested or rural areas have been questioned, and some argue that the funds could be better spent on supporting displaced residents and revitalizing evacuated areas.

The government's support for displaced residents has included compensation payments, assistance with housing, and health care services. However, these initiatives have faced criticism over delays, insufficient support, and for the stress caused by the uncertainty over the long-term plans for evacuated areas.

Nuclear Energy Policy

POST-FUKUSHIMA, THE government has struggled to balance the public's heightened fear of nuclear power with the country's energy needs. All of Japan's nuclear reactors were temporarily shut down following the disaster, causing a significant energy gap that had to be filled by expensive fossil fuel imports.

Despite public opposition, the government has gradually moved towards restarting some of the country's nuclear reactors, under more stringent safety regulations. This policy has been contentious and demonstrates the broader challenges Japan faces in balancing energy security, economic efficiency, and environmental sustainability.

In sum, the Japanese government's handling of the Fukushima Daiichi disaster has had significant successes but also faced numerous challenges. The disaster underscored the importance of effective crisis communication, the need for robust support systems for disaster victims, and the complexities of managing a transition in energy policy in the aftermath of a nuclear disaster.

Criticisms and Investigations into Regulatory Oversight

IN THE WAKE OF THE Fukushima Daiichi disaster, there were significant criticisms and investigations into the regulatory oversight of Japan's nuclear industry. The disaster raised questions about the preparedness of the plant, the adequacy of safety measures, and the response to the crisis, prompting a series of investigations and leading to major regulatory reforms.

Criticisms

THE MAIN CRITICISMS focused on three areas:

1. Lack of Preparedness: Despite Japan's known vulnerability to earthquakes and tsunamis, the Fukushima Daiichi plant was inadequately prepared for the scale of the March 11 disaster. The seawall designed to protect the plant from tsunamis was significantly lower than the wave that hit the plant. The backup power generators, crucial for maintaining the cooling of the reactors in the event of a loss of power, were located in a flood-prone area.

2. Inadequate Safety Culture: Investigations revealed a complacent attitude towards safety within TEPCO and the broader nuclear industry, which prioritized cost-saving and operational efficiency over robust safety measures.

3. Regulatory Failures: The Nuclear and Industrial Safety Agency (NISA), the nuclear regulatory body at the time of the disaster, was a part of the Ministry of Economy, Trade, and Industry (METI), which is responsible for promoting the nuclear industry. This was viewed as a conflict of interest that compromised NISA's ability to regulate the industry effectively. In addition, NISA was criticized for lacking the necessary independence, expertise, and resources to fulfill its mandate effectively.

Investigations

SEVERAL INVESTIGATIONS were launched in the aftermath of the disaster, including the government's Investigation Committee on the Accident at the Fukushima Nuclear Power Stations, the National Diet of Japan's Fukushima Nuclear Accident Independent Investigation Commission, and TEPCO's own investigation.

These investigations highlighted systemic failures in both the nuclear industry and its regulatory oversight. They revealed shortcomings in the design and safety measures at the Fukushima Daiichi plant, the crisis management in response to the disaster, and the regulatory system overseeing nuclear power in Japan.

Regulatory Reforms

THE CRITICISMS AND findings of these investigations led to significant regulatory reforms. In 2012, the Nuclear Regulation Authority (NRA) was established, replacing NISA. The NRA was designed to be more independent, with a mandate separate from the promotion of nuclear energy and was given increased resources and authority. It also implemented new safety standards, considered to be among the world's most stringent.

However, these reforms have not been without controversy, and debates about the safety and future of nuclear power in Japan continue.

In summary, the Fukushima Daiichi disaster exposed significant weaknesses in Japan's nuclear regulatory system and led to major reforms. It underscored the importance of robust, independent regulatory oversight and a strong safety culture in the nuclear industry.

Chapter 9: Lessons Learned: Improving Nuclear Safety

Reevaluating Safety Protocols and Regulatory Frameworks

The Fukushima Daiichi disaster served as a wake-up call to the nuclear industry worldwide, prompting a thorough reevaluation of safety protocols and regulatory frameworks.

Safety Protocols

FOLLOWING THE DISASTER, nuclear facilities around the world reassessed their safety measures, particularly regarding protection against natural disasters. These assessments took into account not just the design specifications of the plants, but also the potential impact of extreme natural events beyond what the plants were originally designed to withstand—a concept known as "beyond design basis" events.

The vulnerability of backup power systems was one key area of focus. These systems are critical for maintaining cooling in the reactors in the event of a power loss, and their failure at Fukushima Daiichi led to the nuclear crisis. Measures such as increasing the height and protection of seawalls, improving the robustness and redundancy of backup power systems, and situating them in elevated, flood-safe locations, have been implemented in many plants.

Another significant area of focus was enhancing the robustness of plant structures to withstand severe natural disasters. This includes strengthening the buildings housing the reactors, spent fuel pools, and other critical structures.

Regulatory Frameworks

THE DISASTER ALSO PROMPTED a reevaluation of regulatory frameworks overseeing nuclear power. In Japan, this led to the establishment of the Nuclear Regulation Authority, designed to be more independent and effective than its predecessor.

Many other countries conducted "stress tests" on their nuclear power plants, reassessing their ability to withstand various disaster scenarios and making improvements where needed.

The International Atomic Energy Agency (IAEA) also played a significant role in reviewing regulatory frameworks and providing guidance. The IAEA's Action Plan on Nuclear Safety, developed in response to the Fukushima disaster, outlined measures to strengthen global nuclear safety, emergency preparedness and response, and regulatory effectiveness.

Crisis Management

THE DISASTER ALSO HIGHLIGHTED the importance of effective crisis management. This includes not just the technical response to a nuclear crisis, but also communication, decision-making, and coordination among various stakeholders. Training and exercises involving different disaster scenarios have become standard in the nuclear industry to prepare for potential emergencies.

The reevaluation of safety protocols and regulatory frameworks following the Fukushima Daiichi disaster led to significant improvements in nuclear safety worldwide. However, the disaster also served as a reminder that safety in the nuclear industry is a continuous process. As technology evolves, as more is learned about the potential risks and impacts of nuclear accidents, and as societal expectations change, safety protocols and regulatory frameworks must continually adapt and improve.

International Cooperation and Sharing Best Practices

THE FUKUSHIMA DAIICHI nuclear disaster underscored the global implications of nuclear accidents and highlighted the importance of international cooperation and sharing best practices within the nuclear industry.

Emergency Response and Recovery

IN THE IMMEDIATE AFTERMATH of the disaster, Japan received assistance from several countries and international organizations. The United States provided considerable aid, including sending experts from the Nuclear Regulatory Commission and Department of Energy, and deploying U.S. Navy assets to assist with the cooling efforts. Other countries, including France and Russia, also sent experts and materials to aid in the crisis.

The International Atomic Energy Agency (IAEA) played a key role in coordinating international assistance, providing technical advice, and disseminating information to the international community. The IAEA also assisted in the recovery phase, providing support for decontamination and decommissioning efforts, and conducting reviews of Japan's stress tests on its other nuclear power plants.

Learning and Sharing Best Practices

THE FUKUSHIMA DISASTER offered a wealth of lessons for nuclear safety, emergency preparedness and response, and regulatory effectiveness. These lessons have been studied and incorporated into best practices worldwide.

For example, the insights gained from the disaster have influenced the design and safety features of new nuclear power plants. Enhancements include passive safety systems, which can operate without human intervention or power supply, and additional robustness against external hazards like earthquakes and tsunamis.

The disaster also underscored the importance of effective crisis communication. Clear, timely, and accurate communication to the public and between organizations and countries is critical during a nuclear emergency. This lesson has been incorporated into emergency response protocols and training programs.

Strengthening International Frameworks

THE FUKUSHIMA DISASTER led to a strengthening of international frameworks for nuclear safety. The IAEA's

Action Plan on Nuclear Safety, developed in response to the disaster, called for the strengthening of the global emergency preparedness and response framework, the enhancement of the IAEA's peer review services, and the strengthening of nuclear safety standards.

In sum, the Fukushima Daiichi nuclear disaster emphasized the importance of international cooperation in both the response to and the learning from nuclear accidents. The disaster has catalyzed improvements in nuclear safety, emergency preparedness, and regulatory effectiveness worldwide, demonstrating the value of sharing experiences and best practices across borders.

68

Chapter 10: Nuclear Power: The Pros and Cons

Exploring the Benefits and Risks Associated with Nuclear Power

Nuclear power, with its potential for high-scale, continuous power generation, represents a significant component of the global energy mix. However, the technology carries with it unique risks, as highlighted by the Fukushima Daiichi disaster. Understanding these benefits and risks is essential for informed decision-making about energy policies.

Benefits of Nuclear Power

1. LOW GREENHOUSE GAS Emissions: Nuclear power produces very low greenhouse gas emissions, comparable to wind and solar power. Given the urgency of addressing climate change, this makes nuclear power an attractive option for low-carbon electricity generation.

2. High Energy Density: Nuclear fission releases approximately one million times more energy per unit mass than fossil fuel sources. This high energy density means that a nuclear power plant requires far less fuel than a comparable coal or gas plant.

3. Reliable, Continuous Power Supply: Unlike intermittent renewable sources such as wind and solar, nuclear power plants can provide a continuous, stable supply of electricity, which is crucial for meeting base load demand.

4. Potential for Technological Advances: Advances in nuclear technology, such as Generation IV reactors and small modular reactors, promise higher efficiency, improved safety features, and solutions to nuclear waste.

Risks of Nuclear Power

1. NUCLEAR ACCIDENTS: While rare, nuclear accidents can have severe, long-lasting impacts on human health and the environment, as demonstrated by the Chernobyl and Fukushima disasters.

2. Nuclear Waste: The disposal of high-level nuclear waste presents a significant challenge. It remains radioactive for thousands of years and requires secure, long-term storage.

3. Nuclear Proliferation: The technology and materials for generating nuclear power can potentially be used to produce nuclear weapons. This risk of nuclear proliferation is a critical concern for global security.

4. High Costs: Building and operating a nuclear power plant is capital-intensive. The costs of decommissioning and waste disposal, as well as the financial liability in case of an accident, make nuclear power an expensive source of electricity.

Balancing the Benefits and Risks

THE BALANCE OF THESE benefits and risks is a subject of ongoing debate. Many countries continue to see nuclear power as a vital part of their energy mix, given its low carbon emissions and reliable power supply. On the other hand, the risks associated with nuclear power, particularly in light of the Fukushima disaster, have led some countries to phase out their nuclear power programs.

While nuclear power presents attractive benefits, particularly in the context of climate change and energy security, it also carries significant risks. The challenge for policy makers is to manage these risks while optimizing the benefits, as part of a diverse, sustainable energy mix.

The Global Debate on Nuclear Energy Post-Fukushima

THE FUKUSHIMA DAIICHI disaster brought the debate on nuclear energy into the global spotlight. While some countries reaffirmed their commitment to nuclear power, considering it essential for meeting climate goals and ensuring energy security, others decided to phase out nuclear power due to safety concerns.

Reaffirming Nuclear Power

IN COUNTRIES LIKE FRANCE, the U.S., China, and Russia, nuclear power remains an integral part of their energy strategies. They argue that nuclear power is a necessary part of the energy mix to provide a stable, low-carbon energy source.

For instance, France, which derives about 70% of its electricity from nuclear energy, continued its commitment to nuclear power, albeit with a renewed emphasis on safety. In the U.S., while no new plants have been commissioned since the disaster, the existing ones continue to operate, some with extended licenses.

China, as part of its ambitious plans to reduce its reliance on coal and cut carbon emissions, is continuing to invest heavily in nuclear power. Russia also continues to expand its nuclear power capacity, both domestically and through exporting its nuclear technology.

Phasing Out Nuclear Power

CONVERSELY, SEVERAL countries decided to phase out nuclear power in response to the Fukushima disaster. Notably, Germany decided to shut down all its nuclear power plants by the end of 2022, a decision known as the "Energiewende" or "energy turnaround". The country plans to replace its nuclear capacity with renewables and improve energy efficiency.

Similarly, Switzerland decided to phase out nuclear power by 2034, and Belgium committed to shutting down its nuclear power plants by 2025. Spain and Taiwan have also set dates for phasing out nuclear power.

The Middle Ground

SOME COUNTRIES HAVE taken a middle path, maintaining their existing nuclear power plants but not planning new ones. For instance, South Korea, despite being one of the most reliant countries on nuclear energy, has declared a policy of "nuclear power reduction".

The Role of Public Opinion

PUBLIC OPINION PLAYS a significant role in shaping these policies. The Fukushima disaster led to an increase in public opposition to nuclear power in many countries due to safety concerns. However, public attitudes vary widely, often influenced by factors such as national energy security concerns, the relative importance of climate change, and trust in regulatory institutions.

The Future of Nuclear Power

THE DEBATE ON NUCLEAR power is likely to continue, particularly in light of the urgent need to address climate change. The development of new technologies, such as small modular reactors and advanced reactor designs, may influence this debate. At the same time, the rapid development and falling costs of renewable energy technologies provide an increasingly viable alternative to nuclear power.

The Fukushima disaster has significantly influenced the global debate on nuclear energy, underlining the importance of nuclear safety and shaping national energy policies. As we move towards a low-carbon future, the role of nuclear power remains a critical and contentious issue.

OLIVER LANCASTER

Chapter 11: Nuclear Energy Policies Worldwide

Overview of Nuclear Energy Policies in Different Countries

Nuclear energy policies vary greatly around the world, shaped by each country's specific energy needs, natural resources, environmental goals, and public opinion. Here's an overview of the nuclear energy policies in several key countries as of my knowledge cutoff in September 2021.

United States

THE U.S. IS HOME TO the largest number of nuclear reactors in the world, providing about 20% of the country's electricity. Despite not commissioning many new plants since the 1980s, the U.S. has extended the licenses of many existing plants. There is no set plan to phase out nuclear power in the U.S., and the technology is seen as a key part of the strategy to reduce greenhouse gas emissions.

France

FRANCE HAS ONE OF THE highest dependencies on nuclear power worldwide, generating around 70% of its electricity from nuclear sources. The French government plans to reduce this reliance to 50% by 2035, replacing some nuclear capacity with renewables. Nevertheless, nuclear energy remains a cornerstone of France's energy strategy.

Germany

IN CONTRAST, GERMANY decided to phase out all nuclear power following the Fukushima disaster. The plan, known as the "Energiewende" or "energy turnaround", includes shutting down all nuclear power plants by the end of 2022, with a shift towards renewable energy and improved energy efficiency.

China

CHINA IS RAPIDLY EXPANDING its nuclear power capacity as part of its strategy to reduce its reliance on coal and lower its carbon emissions. As of 2021, China has the most reactors under construction worldwide and plans to continue this expansion.

Russia

RUSSIA IS ALSO EXPANDING its nuclear power capacity, both domestically and by exporting its nuclear technology. Nuclear power forms a significant part of Russia's electricity generation and is seen as vital for the country's energy security.

Japan

FOLLOWING THE FUKUSHIMA disaster, Japan temporarily shut down all its nuclear reactors. As of 2021, a few have been restarted under new safety standards, but public opposition to nuclear power remains high. The Japanese government's policy includes maintaining nuclear power as part of the energy mix, but the future of nuclear power in Japan is uncertain.

South Korea

SOUTH KOREA RELIES heavily on nuclear power, but in recent years it has declared a policy of "nuclear power reduction". This includes plans to not build new nuclear power plants and to phase out some of the existing ones, with a shift towards renewable energy.

While nuclear energy policies vary greatly worldwide, they all reflect the ongoing debate over the risks and benefits of nuclear power. The future of nuclear power will depend on various factors, including technological advancements, energy needs, climate change goals, and public opinion.

Changes and Adjustments Made Following the Fukushima Disaster

THE FUKUSHIMA DAIICHI nuclear disaster spurred a global reassessment of nuclear safety, emergency preparedness, and regulatory oversight, leading to significant changes and adjustments in the nuclear industry and related policies.

Strengthening Safety Measures

ONE OF THE IMMEDIATE actions post-Fukushima was to review and strengthen safety measures at nuclear facilities. This included upgrading infrastructure to withstand extreme natural disasters, improving the robustness and redundancy of backup power systems, and enhancing the containment of radiation.

Nuclear power plants worldwide underwent "stress tests" to evaluate their ability to withstand various disaster scenarios. Based on the results, plants implemented necessary improvements.

Countries located in seismic zones or with coastlines exposed to tsunamis, in particular, reassessed the risk and protection measures against these hazards. The disaster highlighted the need to consider "beyond design basis" events - scenarios not initially considered in the plant's design.

Enhancing Emergency Preparedness

FUKUSHIMA UNDERSCORED the importance of being prepared for a nuclear emergency. This includes not just the technical aspects of managing a nuclear crisis but also communication, decision-making, and coordination among various stakeholders.

Emergency response protocols were revised to include lessons learned from Fukushima. Training and exercises involving different disaster scenarios have become standard in the nuclear industry, enhancing readiness for potential emergencies.

Regulatory Reforms

THE DISASTER EXPOSED weaknesses in Japan's nuclear regulatory system and led to significant reforms. The newly established Nuclear Regulation Authority was designed to be more independent, robust, and transparent than its predecessor. It implemented new safety standards that are among the world's most stringent.

Other countries also strengthened their nuclear regulatory frameworks, incorporating lessons from Fukushima. There was a broader shift towards enhancing the independence and effectiveness of nuclear regulators and emphasizing a strong safety culture in the nuclear industry.

Policy Adjustments

IN RESPONSE TO FUKUSHIMA, some countries decided to phase out nuclear power, including Germany, Switzerland, and Belgium. These countries have shifted their focus to renewable energy and energy efficiency.

In contrast, others like France, the U.S., China, and Russia, reaffirmed their commitment to nuclear power, albeit with a renewed emphasis on safety. The disaster sparked public debates about the use of nuclear energy, shaping energy policies in many countries.

International Cooperation

FUKUSHIMA UNDERSCORED the global implications of nuclear accidents, leading to enhanced international cooperation in nuclear safety. This includes information sharing, joint research, peer reviews, and coordinated emergency response.

The Fukushima disaster has led to significant changes and adjustments in the nuclear industry worldwide, enhancing nuclear safety, emergency preparedness, and regulatory oversight. The disaster served as a stark reminder of the risks associated with nuclear power and the importance of continuous learning and improvement in managing these risks.

FUKUSHIMA FALLOUT: UNVEILING THE TRUTH BEHIND THE 2011 NUCLEAR DISASTER

Chapter 12: Nuclear Decommissioning: The Road to Recovery

The Challenges and Complexities of Decommissioning the Fukushima Plant

Decommissioning a nuclear power plant is a complex and challenging process under normal circumstances. However, the decommissioning of the Fukushima Daiichi plant, severely damaged by the 2011 disaster, presents a set of unique challenges and complexities.

High Levels of Radiation

ONE OF THE MOST SIGNIFICANT challenges in decommissioning the Fukushima plant is dealing with high levels of radiation. The radiation levels in certain parts of the reactors are so high that they could be fatal to humans within a short period. This makes direct human intervention impossible in these areas and complicates the decommissioning process.

Location and Condition of Melted Fuel

A CRITICAL ASPECT OF the decommissioning process is the removal of the melted nuclear fuel, also known as corium. However, the exact location and condition of this fuel in the reactors is unknown. This uncertainty adds to the complexity of planning for its removal.

Development and Deployment of Technology

GIVEN THE HIGH RADIATION levels and uncertainty about the fuel's location, special technology must be developed and deployed for the decommissioning process. This includes remote-controlled robots capable of withstanding high radiation levels and navigating the damaged reactor buildings.

Management of Radioactive Waste

ANOTHER MAJOR CHALLENGE is the management of radioactive waste generated during decommissioning. This includes spent fuel, contaminated water used to cool the reactors, and contaminated materials removed from the site. The long-term storage and disposal of this waste require careful planning and robust solutions to protect human health and the environment.

Long Timeframe

DECOMMISSIONING A DAMAGED nuclear power plant is a long-term process. The decommissioning of the Fukushima plant is expected to take several decades. Managing such a long-term project presents challenges in terms of maintaining expertise, resources, and public trust over an extended period.

Cost

THE COST OF DECOMMISSIONING the Fukushima plant is enormous, estimated to be several tens of billions of dollars. Managing this cost and determining who should bear it is a significant challenge.

The decommissioning of the Fukushima Daiichi plant is a highly complex and challenging process that will continue for decades. It requires technical expertise, careful planning, long-term commitment, and substantial resources. The lessons learned from this process will likely inform decommissioning practices and policies worldwide.

Efforts Towards Decontamination and Future Plans for the Site

DECONTAMINATION AND revitalization of the Fukushima Daiichi site and surrounding areas is an immense task, requiring meticulous planning, substantial resources, and long-term commitment.

Decontamination Efforts

THE DECONTAMINATION process involves removing radioactive materials from the environment. This can include tasks like cleaning roofs and roads, removing topsoil, and cutting down vegetation. In some cases, whole buildings may need to be demolished.

Decontamination work in the evacuation zones surrounding the plant started soon after the disaster, focusing on residential areas, farmland, and infrastructure. The aim was to reduce the radiation levels so that residents could safely return to their homes.

One significant challenge has been the disposal of contaminated soil and waste. Temporary storage sites were created to hold this material until a permanent disposal solution is found. As of my last training cut-off in September 2021, discussions regarding the final disposal method for this contaminated waste are ongoing.

Future Plans for the Site

THE FUTURE PLANS FOR the Fukushima Daiichi site are closely linked with the decommissioning process. Given the long timeline for decommissioning, the site will remain an industrial zone for several decades.

One proposal for the site's future is to construct a research and development facility. This facility could focus on areas such as nuclear decommissioning technology and renewable energy, turning the site into a symbol of regeneration and progress.

Another aspect of future planning involves the treated but still radioactive water stored at the plant. As of 2021, the Japanese government has decided to release this water into the sea, after further treatment to reduce the radioactive content below regulatory limits. This decision is subject to stringent safety and environmental assessments and is being undertaken in consultation with the International Atomic Energy Agency (IAEA).

FUKUSHIMA FALLOUT: UNVEILING THE TRUTH BEHIND THE 2011 NUCLEAR DISASTER

The decontamination and future planning for the Fukushima site represent a significant effort towards recovery and revitalization. While progress has been made, significant challenges remain. The process is a long-term commitment, demanding continuous engagement with a wide range of stakeholders, including local residents, scientists, policymakers, and international organizations.

Chapter 13: The Human Side of the Disaster: Personal Stories

Stories of Individuals Directly Impacted by the Disaster

The Fukushima Daiichi disaster had profound, life-altering impacts on many individuals, forever changing the fabric of their lives. From workers at the plant to local residents, the disaster brought about experiences of loss, resilience, and a shared sense of community.

Plant Workers and First Responders

THE WORKERS AT THE Fukushima Daiichi plant, along with the firefighters, Self-Defense Forces personnel, and others who responded to the crisis, were the frontline heroes. They braved high radiation levels, explosions, and the uncertainty of a nuclear disaster to bring the situation under control. The workers, often referred to as the "Fukushima 50," faced not only physical danger but also psychological stress.

Local Residents

FOR THE RESIDENTS OF Fukushima, the disaster brought sudden and dramatic changes. Tens of thousands of people were forced to evacuate their homes, leaving behind their belongings, and in many cases, their livelihoods. The disruption caused by the evacuation, uncertainty about the future, and fear of radiation had significant psychological impacts, sometimes referred to as "nuclear anxiety".

Some residents have chosen to return to their homes in the areas where the evacuation orders have been lifted, facing the challenge of rebuilding their lives and communities. Others have decided to start anew elsewhere, sometimes due to concerns about radiation, changes in their life situations, or the desire for a stable future.

Farmers and Fishermen

FARMERS AND FISHERMEN from the Fukushima region were severely affected by the disaster. Despite their efforts to decontaminate the land and sea, and rigorous safety checks on their produce, they have struggled to overcome fears and misconceptions about radiation, affecting their livelihoods.

Younger Generation

FOR THE YOUNGER GENERATION who grew up in the shadow of the disaster, the impacts are multifaceted. While they have had to grapple with disruptions to their normal life and concerns about radiation, they have also been at the forefront of creating a new narrative for Fukushima, one of resilience and hope.

These individual stories highlight the human impact of the Fukushima disaster. The event underscored not only the importance of physical safety measures but also the need for psychological care and community support in the aftermath of such a catastrophe. The experiences of these individuals remind us of the strength of the human spirit and our collective capacity for resilience in the face of adversity.

Voices of Survivors, Evacuees, and Affected Communities

THE VOICES OF SURVIVORS, evacuees, and affected communities of the Fukushima disaster offer deep, personal insights into the human experience of such an event. Their stories speak of loss, resilience, community, and hope, forming a poignant narrative of the disaster's impacts.

Survivors' Testimonies

SURVIVORS OF THE DISASTER often share stories of the harrowing moments when the earthquake and tsunami hit, the confusion and fear that ensued, and the immense challenges of evacuation. Many speak of the emotional trauma of leaving behind homes, possessions, and a familiar way of life in the face of an invisible threat - radiation.

Challenges Faced by Evacuees

EVACUEES TALK ABOUT the challenges of life post-evacuation. These include the difficulty of living in temporary housing, the stress and anxiety over radiation exposure, and the pain of being separated from home and community. They also express concern about the stigma associated with being an evacuee from Fukushima, rooted in misunderstandings about radiation.

Despite these hardships, many evacuees also speak of resilience. They discuss the support they received from each other, from volunteers, and from host communities. They share stories of forging new connections, developing new skills, and gradually rebuilding their lives.

Voices from the Affected Communities

COMMUNITY VOICES OFTEN highlight the social impacts of the disaster. They speak about the fragmentation of communities due to evacuation, the challenge of maintaining community bonds and traditions, and the concern over the depopulation of affected areas, particularly by the younger generation.

Farmers and fishermen talk about their efforts to decontaminate their land and sea, the rigorous safety checks they undertake, and their struggle to restore consumer confidence. They express their determination to continue their livelihoods and maintain the traditions of their communities.

Younger Voices

THE VOICES OF THE YOUNGER generation reflect a range of experiences and perspectives. Some express anxiety over radiation and the changes brought about by the disaster. Others speak about their efforts to overcome adversity, their desire to contribute to their communities, and their hopes for the future.

Many young people have become active in various initiatives - from radiation monitoring and renewable energy projects to community-building activities - becoming agents of change in the post-Fukushima context.

Listening to the voices of survivors, evacuees, and affected communities is crucial for understanding the full impact of the Fukushima disaster and for informing recovery efforts. Their experiences and perspectives remind us of the enduring human capacity to face adversity, to rebuild, and to envision a different future.

94

Chapter 14: Socioeconomic Consequences: Economic Impact and Recovery

---

Assessing the Economic Impact on the Region and Japan as a Whole

The Fukushima disaster had significant economic impacts, both in the immediate region and on Japan as a whole. These impacts spanned various sectors and had both short-term and long-term implications.

Direct Economic Losses

DIRECT ECONOMIC LOSSES from the disaster included damage to the Fukushima Daiichi plant itself and to the surrounding infrastructure. The cost of the ongoing decommissioning process, estimated to take several decades, is substantial and continues to grow.

Compensation and Decontamination Costs

A SIGNIFICANT ECONOMIC burden came from compensation payments to evacuees and businesses affected by the disaster. As of my last training cut-off in September 2021, these payments were still ongoing. The costs of decontamination efforts in the affected areas were also significant.

Impact on Local Economy

THE LOCAL ECONOMY OF Fukushima was heavily impacted. Agriculture, forestry, and fisheries sectors, once thriving in the region, were severely affected due to concerns over radioactive contamination. Despite rigorous safety checks and decontamination efforts, these sectors have struggled to recover fully due to persistent fears and misconceptions about radiation.

Many small and medium-sized enterprises, particularly in the evacuation zones, suffered severe losses. The tourism sector also faced a major setback.

Energy Costs

WITH THE SHUTDOWN OF all nuclear power plants after the disaster, Japan had to rely more heavily on fossil fuel imports for electricity generation. This resulted in increased energy costs and affected Japan's trade balance.

Macro-Economic Impact

AT THE NATIONAL LEVEL, the disaster led to a contraction in economic output in the short term. However, reconstruction and decontamination efforts provided a stimulus in subsequent years.

The long-term macro-economic impact is more complex to assess. It includes factors such as the changed energy policies, increased disaster risk awareness and preparedness, and the costs of health care and support for affected populations.

Impact on Foreign Investments and Trade

THE DISASTER AND THE ensuing nuclear crisis raised concerns among foreign investors and trading partners in the short term. While these concerns have largely abated over time, certain sectors like food exports from the region continue to face challenges due to concerns over radioactive contamination.

The economic impact of the Fukushima disaster is profound and multifaceted. While some costs can be quantified, others, such as the impact on the social fabric of affected communities, the mental health of the population, and the loss of trust in nuclear power, are harder to measure. The disaster underscores the economic as well as the human cost of major nuclear accidents.

Strategies for Revitalization and Rebuilding Affected Areas

THE REVITALIZATION and rebuilding of areas affected by the Fukushima disaster is a monumental task. The process requires a comprehensive, long-term strategy that addresses not just physical reconstruction but also social, economic, and psychological recovery. Here are some of the key strategies being pursued.

Decontamination and Infrastructure Rebuilding

ONE OF THE FIRST STEPS towards revitalization is decontamination, which involves removing radioactive materials from the environment. This task, although colossal, is crucial for making the affected areas safe for habitation again.

Simultaneously, efforts have been made to rebuild infrastructure, such as homes, roads, schools, and hospitals, that were damaged or destroyed by the earthquake, tsunami, and subsequent nuclear disaster.

Economic Revitalization

REVITALIZING THE LOCAL economy is key to the recovery process. This includes supporting traditional industries such as agriculture, forestry, and fisheries, which have been severely affected by fears of radiation.

Initiatives have also been taken to attract new industries to the area, including renewable energy and robotics. In addition, there are plans to develop the decommissioned Fukushima plant into a research and development hub, creating jobs and attracting investments.

Community Reconstruction

REBUILDING COMMUNITIES goes beyond physical reconstruction; it requires restoring social bonds, local culture, and community activities. Efforts have been made to support community-based initiatives, provide social spaces, and organize events to help foster a sense of community among residents.

Health and Well-being Support

GIVEN THE PSYCHOLOGICAL impacts of the disaster, support for mental health and well-being is a crucial part of the recovery process. This includes providing counseling services, community health programs, and ongoing health monitoring.

Public Participation and Communication

PUBLIC PARTICIPATION is key to the revitalization process. It's important that residents have a say in the planning and decision-making processes that shape their communities' future. Transparent and regular communication is also crucial to building trust and providing reassurance about safety measures.

Reputation Management

ADDRESSING THE NEGATIVE image associated with Fukushima, due to the nuclear disaster, is also a part of the recovery strategy. This involves rigorous safety checks, transparent reporting, and initiatives to promote the region's produce, tourism, and other attractions.

The revitalization and rebuilding of the areas affected by the Fukushima disaster is a complex, long-term process. It requires not only resources and technical expertise but also resilience, participation, and the shared vision of the residents. The strategies pursued hold lessons for recovery efforts from similar disasters worldwide.

Chapter 15: Alternative Energy Sources: Exploring Sustainable Options

Advancements in Renewable Energy Technologies

Renewable energy technologies have seen significant advancements over the past decade. These developments are contributing to the global transition towards sustainable, low-carbon energy systems.

Solar Power

ADVANCEMENTS IN SOLAR photovoltaic (PV) technology have resulted in higher efficiency panels, making solar power more competitive with traditional power sources. Concentrated solar power (CSP), which uses mirrors or lenses to concentrate sunlight onto a small area to generate heat, has also seen important advancements, including the development of more efficient and cost-effective thermal storage systems.

Solar technology has also expanded beyond solar farms and rooftop panels. Innovations include solar windows, solar-powered vehicles, and even solar roads. The advent of "floating solar" technology allows for installations on water bodies, increasing the range of locations where solar energy can be harnessed.

Wind Power

WIND POWER TECHNOLOGY has also improved significantly. The size and efficiency of wind turbines have increased, resulting in lower costs and making wind power a viable option for many regions. Offshore wind power, in particular, has seen significant advancements, with larger turbines and improved installation and maintenance techniques.

There have also been developments in small-scale wind turbines for use in urban settings, and in airborne wind energy systems that harness the wind at higher altitudes where it is stronger and more consistent.

Hydropower

WHILE HYDROPOWER IS a mature technology, advancements continue to be made, particularly in the development of small-scale, run-of-river installations that have a lesser environmental impact compared to large-scale dams.

Energy Storage

ENERGY STORAGE IS A crucial component of a renewable-powered grid, as it can help to balance supply and demand and manage the intermittent nature of solar and wind power. The most notable advancements have been in battery technology, with the development of more efficient, cheaper, and longer-lasting batteries.

Pumped hydro storage, thermal storage, and other forms of large-scale energy storage have also seen advancements. Additionally, the development of smart grid technology, which can dynamically manage supply and demand, is an important complement to energy storage.

Other Technologies

OTHER RENEWABLE TECHNOLOGIES, such as geothermal and tidal energy, have also seen advancements, although they are currently less widely adopted. Bioenergy has seen innovations in the use of algae and advanced biofuels.

The advancements in renewable energy technologies are a key enabler of the global transition to sustainable energy systems. These technologies continue to evolve, and further innovations are anticipated in the coming years, making renewable energy more accessible, efficient, and cost-effective.

The Role of Alternative Energy Sources in Reducing Dependence on Nuclear Power

ALTERNATIVE ENERGY sources, particularly renewables, play a crucial role in reducing dependence on nuclear power. As the world seeks to transition to a more sustainable, low-carbon energy future, these sources offer viable, environmentally friendly alternatives to nuclear power.

Solar Power

SOLAR POWER HAS SEEN significant growth in recent years, driven by advancements in photovoltaic technology and decreases in cost. Solar energy has the advantage of being abundant, clean, and widely available. Large-scale solar farms and small-scale rooftop panels can generate electricity for the grid, homes, businesses, and remote areas, contributing to a diversified and resilient energy mix.

Wind Power

WIND POWER IS ANOTHER rapidly growing sector. Wind farms, both onshore and offshore, can generate large amounts of electricity. Like solar power, wind is a clean and renewable source of energy. Advanced wind turbines are more efficient and capable of generating power even with low wind speeds, increasing the potential locations where wind energy can be harnessed.

Hydropower

HYDROPOWER, A LONG-established source of renewable energy, continues to play a significant role in many countries' energy mixes. While large-scale hydropower projects can have environmental and social impacts, small-scale and run-of-river installations can generate electricity with lesser impacts.

Bioenergy

BIOENERGY, DERIVED from organic materials, can serve as a source of heat, electricity, and transport fuel. It has the advantage of being storable and can provide energy continuously, unlike the intermittent nature of solar and wind power.

Geothermal Energy

GEOTHERMAL ENERGY, which harnesses the heat from the earth, can provide a stable, continuous source of electricity and heating. While the potential for geothermal energy is location-dependent, in certain regions it can be a significant contributor to the energy mix.

Energy Storage and Smart Grids

ALTERNATIVE ENERGY sources are often complemented by energy storage systems, such as batteries, pumped hydro storage, or thermal storage. These systems can store excess energy produced during periods of high wind or sunlight for use when conditions are less favorable.

Smart grid technology also plays a role in managing the variable nature of some renewable sources. Smart grids can adjust demand in real-time, integrate various sources of energy, and improve the reliability and efficiency of the power system.

Alternative energy sources have a crucial role to play in reducing dependence on nuclear power. A diversified energy mix, incorporating different forms of renewable energy, along with energy storage and smart grids, can provide a stable, sustainable, and low-carbon solution for our energy needs.

Chapter 16: Nuclear Diplomacy: International Cooperation and Concerns

Global Response to the Fukushima Disaster

The Fukushima disaster prompted a significant global response, reflecting the international implications of such an event. The response was multifaceted, spanning humanitarian aid, nuclear safety, regulatory reforms, and changes in energy policy.

Immediate Humanitarian Response

IN THE IMMEDIATE AFTERMATH of the disaster, international aid poured into Japan to help with the humanitarian crisis caused by the earthquake and tsunami. Countries around the world offered financial aid, supplies, rescue teams, and other forms of assistance.

International Atomic Energy Agency (IAEA) Involvement

THE INTERNATIONAL ATOMIC Energy Agency (IAEA) played a crucial role in the international response. The IAEA offered technical support to Japan, coordinated international assistance, and gathered and disseminated information about the nuclear emergency.

The IAEA also conducted multiple reviews of Japan's actions and response, providing recommendations for improvement. These reviews contributed to a better understanding of the disaster and informed changes in nuclear safety worldwide.

Nuclear Safety and Regulatory Reforms

THE FUKUSHIMA DISASTER led to a global reassessment of nuclear safety. Countries with nuclear power plants conducted "stress tests" to assess their ability to withstand extreme natural disasters. Many countries revised their regulatory frameworks, made safety upgrades at their nuclear facilities, and enhanced their emergency preparedness measures.

Changes in Energy Policy

THE DISASTER HAD A significant impact on global energy policies. Some countries, like Germany, Switzerland, and Belgium, decided to phase out nuclear power. Others, particularly those heavily reliant on nuclear power, reaffirmed their commitment but with a renewed emphasis on safety.

Public Debate and Activism

THE FUKUSHIMA DISASTER sparked a global debate on the use of nuclear energy and led to heightened activism against nuclear power. Public opposition to nuclear power increased in many countries, influencing energy policies and leading to protests and other actions.

International Research and Cooperation

THE DISASTER UNDERSCORED the importance of international cooperation in nuclear safety. This includes sharing information and best practices, conducting joint research, and coordinating emergency preparedness and response.

The global response to the Fukushima disaster reflects the international community's shared concern over nuclear safety. The disaster served as a stark reminder of the potential risks of nuclear power, prompting a global reassessment of nuclear safety measures, regulatory frameworks, and energy policies.

Diplomatic Implications and Implications for Nuclear Non-Proliferation Efforts

THE FUKUSHIMA DISASTER, while primarily a safety and humanitarian crisis, also had diplomatic implications and affected nuclear non-proliferation efforts.

Diplomatic Implications

AS AN EVENT WITH TRANSBOUNDARY impacts, the Fukushima disaster necessitated international cooperation. This event reinforced the crucial role of diplomacy and international organizations, such as the International Atomic

Energy Agency (IAEA), in coordinating emergency response, disseminating information, and guiding safety improvements.

Countries with nuclear technology, like the U.S., France, Russia, and China, had to engage in diplomatic communications with countries that were reassessing their nuclear power plans after Fukushima. Assurances over safety standards, technology sharing for improved safeguards, and cooperation on nuclear regulation were important diplomatic activities in the post-Fukushima context.

In Japan, the government's handling of the crisis and its decision-making around issues like the discharge of treated radioactive water into the Pacific Ocean had diplomatic ramifications, particularly with its neighbors like South Korea and China.

Implications for Nuclear Non-Proliferation Efforts

THE FUKUSHIMA DISASTER underscored the risks associated with nuclear technology, adding a new dimension to nuclear non-proliferation efforts. While non-proliferation primarily focuses on preventing the spread of nuclear weapons, the disaster highlighted the necessity of stringent safety standards to prevent nuclear accidents.

Nuclear power states, while reassuring the safety of nuclear energy, also had to address concerns about the security of nuclear materials and facilities. The disaster emphasized the importance of regulatory oversight, not only for safety but also for security against potential misuse of nuclear materials or acts of terrorism.

The disaster also fed into the debate about the civilian use of nuclear energy in countries seeking to develop nuclear power capabilities. It underscored the importance of robust safety infrastructure and regulatory systems, alongside commitments to non-proliferation.

The Fukushima disaster highlighted the interconnectedness of the issues of nuclear power, safety, and non-proliferation. It underscored the need for robust international frameworks, diplomatic engagement, and transparency in dealing with these issues. The event added a layer of complexity to the diplomatic landscape around nuclear technology, influencing discussions on nuclear safety, non-proliferation, and the future of nuclear energy.

Chapter 17: Remembering Fukushima: Memorials and Lessons for the Future

---

Commemorating the Victims and Honoring Their Memory

The Fukushima disaster left a profound impact, leading to loss of lives, displacement of communities, and lasting changes in the region. Commemorating the victims and honoring their memory is an important part of acknowledging this tragedy and the resilience of those affected.

Memorial Services

EACH YEAR, MEMORIAL services are held on March 11th to mark the anniversary of the disaster. These services, attended by survivors, families of the victims, first responders, government officials, and representatives from across Japan, are a time for collective mourning and remembrance. They are also a moment to honor the bravery and sacrifices of those who responded to the crisis.

Monuments and Memorials

SEVERAL MONUMENTS AND memorials have been erected in honor of the victims. These installations serve as a lasting reminder of the disaster and its consequences. One such monument is the "Miracle Pine," a single tree that survived the tsunami in Rikuzentakata and has been preserved as a symbol of hope and resilience.

Plans have also been proposed for a memorial park in the area, offering a space for contemplation and remembrance.

Museums and Exhibitions

MUSEUMS AND EXHIBITIONS dedicated to the disaster play a crucial role in honoring the memory of the victims. They provide a space to educate visitors about the events of March 11th, the response to the disaster, and its ongoing impacts.

For instance, the Great East Japan Earthquake and Nuclear Disaster Memorial Museum in Futaba town offer exhibitions on the disaster and recovery efforts, preserving the history for future generations.

Personal Testimonies and Stories

COLLECTING AND SHARING personal testimonies and stories from survivors and those affected by the disaster is another way of honoring the victims' memory. These narratives provide a deeply human perspective on the disaster, preserving individual experiences, and promoting understanding and empathy.

Commemorating the victims of the Fukushima disaster and honoring their memory is an essential part of the healing process. It helps to preserve the history of the event, provides a space for collective mourning and remembrance, and pays tribute to the resilience and courage of the communities affected. Through these commemorations, the lessons of the disaster continue to resonate, reminding us of the human cost of such events and the importance of preventing similar tragedies in the future.

Ensuring that the Lessons from Fukushima Shape Future Decision-Making

THE FUKUSHIMA DISASTER has provided critical lessons for the world, with far-reaching implications for nuclear safety, emergency preparedness, energy policy, and community resilience. Ensuring these lessons shape future decision-making is crucial for preventing similar catastrophes and building a safer and more sustainable future.

Improving Nuclear Safety and Emergency Preparedness

ONE OF THE KEY LESSONS from Fukushima is the necessity of robust nuclear safety measures. Future decision-making in nuclear power must involve continually reassessing and enhancing safety systems, considering extreme and unexpected disaster scenarios, and ensuring the robustness of backup systems.

Enhanced emergency preparedness is another crucial area. This includes improving disaster response protocols, conducting regular drills and stress-tests, training personnel in managing crisis scenarios, and ensuring clear communication during emergencies.

Reforming Regulatory Frameworks

THE DISASTER EXPOSED gaps in nuclear regulatory oversight, underscoring the need for independent, strong, and transparent regulatory bodies. Future decision-making should involve continued reforms in regulatory frameworks, with a focus on maintaining high safety standards and fostering a culture of safety within the nuclear industry.

Considering Energy Policies

THE FUKUSHIMA DISASTER has sparked worldwide debates on energy policies. It has led some countries to scale back or abandon their nuclear power programs, whereas others have reaffirmed their commitment to nuclear power with reinforced safety measures.

The lessons from Fukushima underscore the importance of diversifying energy sources, enhancing energy efficiency, and investing in renewable energy technologies. Future decision-making must take into account not just economic considerations, but also safety, environmental impact, and social acceptability.

Building Resilient Communities

FUKUSHIMA ALSO OFFERS lessons on the importance of community resilience in the face of disasters. Future decision-making in disaster-prone regions should prioritize community-based disaster risk reduction strategies, local capacity building, and public participation in decision-making processes.

Promoting Transparency and Communication

THE HANDLING OF THE Fukushima disaster highlighted the importance of transparency and clear communication in managing crises. Future decision-making should prioritize open dialogue with the public, regular updates during crisis situations, and education to ensure accurate public understanding of complex issues like radiation risk.

The lessons from the Fukushima disaster are a stark reminder of the potential risks associated with nuclear power and the importance of robust safety measures, regulatory oversight, and emergency preparedness. Ensuring these lessons shape future decision-making is crucial for reducing the risks of similar disasters, promoting sustainable energy policies, and fostering resilient communities.

Chapter 18: The Aftermath: Legal and Ethical Considerations

Legal Ramifications and Compensation for Victims

The Fukushima disaster had serious legal ramifications, involving compensation for victims, lawsuits against the responsible entities, and regulatory changes to prevent future incidents. These legal processes have played a vital role in seeking justice for victims and promoting accountability.

Compensation for Victims

UNDER JAPANESE LAW, the operator of the nuclear power plant, Tokyo Electric Power Company (TEPCO), was liable for compensation to the victims of the disaster. This included payments to individuals and businesses affected by evacuation orders, the loss of livelihoods due to radiation, and other damages.

The compensation process has been complex and lengthy, with ongoing disputes over the amount of damages and the assessment of claims. By my last training cut-off in September 2021, billions of dollars had been paid out, and payments were still continuing.

Lawsuits

SEVERAL LAWSUITS HAVE been filed against TEPCO and the Japanese government by victims of the disaster. These lawsuits have claimed negligence in the construction and operation of the Fukushima plant, failure to take adequate safety measures against a large tsunami, and shortcomings in the response to the crisis.

The legal proceedings have been important for establishing responsibility for the disaster, providing some redress for victims, and pushing for safety improvements in the nuclear industry.

Regulatory Changes

IN RESPONSE TO THE disaster, Japan made significant changes to its nuclear regulatory framework. A new regulatory body, the Nuclear Regulation Authority (NRA), was established, with a mandate to enforce stricter safety standards, conduct rigorous inspections, and promote a safety culture in the nuclear industry.

These changes were aimed at addressing the regulatory shortcomings exposed by the disaster and ensuring that nuclear power plants in Japan are better prepared to withstand severe disasters in the future.

The legal ramifications of the Fukushima disaster have been a crucial part of the response to the crisis. Through compensation payments, lawsuits, and regulatory changes, the legal process has sought to provide some redress for victims, promote accountability, and push for improvements in nuclear safety.

Ethical Dilemmas Surrounding Nuclear Energy and Responsibility

THE FUKUSHIMA DISASTER, like other nuclear accidents, raises several ethical dilemmas surrounding the use of nuclear energy and questions of responsibility. These dilemmas are complex and multifaceted, involving considerations of risk, justice, transparency, and future generations.

Risk and Precaution

THE USE OF NUCLEAR energy involves a balance between the benefits of a low-carbon, high-capacity power source and the risks of severe accidents and long-lived radioactive waste. How we balance these considerations is an ethical question, involving values of precaution, risk tolerance, and sustainability.

Inter-generational Justice

THE LONG-LIVED NATURE of radioactive waste raises ethical questions about inter-generational justice. Are we justified in using a technology that benefits us now but poses risks and burdens for future generations? This question becomes even more acute in the wake of a disaster like Fukushima, which vividly illustrates the potential costs of nuclear energy.

Transparency and Trust

THE HANDLING OF INFORMATION during a nuclear crisis also raises ethical issues. Transparency, truthfulness, and the timely communication of risks are key ethical responsibilities. The Fukushima disaster has raised concerns about how these responsibilities were met, highlighting the importance of trust in institutions and experts.

Responsibility and Compensation

DETERMINING RESPONSIBILITY for nuclear accidents is another complex ethical issue. While legal responsibility may lie with the plant operator, there are broader ethical questions about the responsibilities of regulators, governments, and the nuclear industry as a whole. The adequacy of compensation for victims, and who bears the cost, are also important ethical considerations.

Public Participation

ETHICAL QUESTIONS ALSO arise about public participation in decisions about nuclear energy. What say should communities have in decisions about the construction or operation of nuclear power plants, especially given the potential risks they face? How should the views of the public be taken into account in energy policy?

The ethical dilemmas surrounding nuclear energy are complex and challenging. They involve deep questions about risk, responsibility, justice, trust, and public participation. The Fukushima disaster has brought these dilemmas into sharp focus, highlighting the need for ongoing dialogue and reflection on the ethics of nuclear energy.

124

Chapter 19: Beyond Fukushima: Looking Ahead to a Safer Tomorrow

Reflections on the Legacy of the Fukushima Disaster

The Fukushima Daiichi nuclear disaster left an indelible mark not only on the affected region but also on the world. Its legacy, intertwined with sorrow, resilience, and profound learnings, continues to influence decisions on energy policy, disaster management, and community rebuilding.

Sorrow and Loss

THE MOST IMMEDIATE and tragic legacy of the Fukushima disaster is the loss it engendered. The loss of life, the displacement of communities, the destruction of landscapes and livelihoods, and the ongoing impact on the health and wellbeing of the affected populations represent a deep and enduring sorrow that should not be forgotten.

Resilience and Recovery

YET, ALONGSIDE SORROW, the disaster also illuminated resilience. The resilience of those who braved the initial crisis, the workers, and first responders who risked their lives to mitigate the disaster. The resilience of displaced individuals and communities who have sought to rebuild their lives amidst uncertainty. And the resilience of a region endeavoring to recover and redefine itself in the wake of such a significant event.

Safety and Accountability

THE DISASTER HAS HAD a profound impact on nuclear safety worldwide. The shortcomings exposed by the crisis prompted countries to reevaluate their safety measures, leading to stricter regulations and more rigorous oversight. The Fukushima disaster has underscored that the responsibility of ensuring safety extends beyond power plant operators to encompass regulatory bodies, government agencies, and indeed, society at large.

Changes in Energy Policy

THE LEGACY OF FUKUSHIMA is also evident in changes to global energy policy. The disaster sparked debates about the role of nuclear energy in a world grappling with the dual challenge of reducing carbon emissions and ensuring energy security. In response, some countries chose to phase out nuclear power, others redoubled their safety efforts, and still others saw renewed urgency in investing in alternative, renewable energy sources.

Community Participation and Transparency

THE CRISIS HIGHLIGHTED the importance of community participation in decision-making processes, particularly those concerning safety and recovery efforts. The demand for greater transparency in the wake of the disaster has influenced policy and practice, stressing the need for clear communication and trust-building in managing nuclear energy and other high-risk technologies.

The legacy of the Fukushima disaster extends beyond the immediate tragedy. Its influence continues to shape nuclear safety protocols, energy policies, disaster preparedness measures, and community resilience strategies. As we reflect on the disaster, it is essential to remember the lessons it has taught us and to ensure they continue to inform our actions to build a safer and more sustainable future.

Steps Taken to Prevent Similar Incidents and Build a Safer Nuclear Future

THE FUKUSHIMA DISASTER was a turning point in understanding the need for enhanced safety measures, stringent regulatory frameworks, and comprehensive disaster preparedness plans to mitigate risks associated with nuclear power. The following steps have been taken globally to prevent similar incidents and build a safer nuclear future.

Upgraded Safety Measures

POST-FUKUSHIMA, NUCLEAR facilities worldwide have been re-evaluated for their safety against severe natural disasters such as earthquakes and tsunamis. Upgrades have been made in physical infrastructure, backup power systems, and cooling systems to ensure they can withstand extreme events.

Regulatory Reforms

REGULATORY REFORMS have been implemented in several countries, strengthening the oversight and enforcement of nuclear safety. For instance, Japan established the Nuclear Regulation Authority (NRA), an independent regulatory body with a mandate to prioritize safety over the promotion of nuclear energy.

Stress Tests

COUNTRIES WITH NUCLEAR power plants have conducted "stress tests" to evaluate their resilience against extreme disasters. These tests examine both the physical robustness of the plant and the effectiveness of emergency procedures, identifying areas of vulnerability and guiding safety improvements.

Enhanced Disaster Preparedness

DISASTER PREPAREDNESS plans have been bolstered to respond effectively to potential nuclear accidents. This includes the training of personnel, establishing clear lines of communication, and devising comprehensive evacuation and containment strategies.

Improved Emergency Response Protocols

EMERGENCY RESPONSE protocols have been revised to ensure prompt, coordinated, and effective action in the event of a crisis. This includes measures for early detection of issues, swift decision-making processes, and robust mechanisms for crisis communication.

Public Participation and Transparency

EFFORTS HAVE BEEN MADE to involve the public more in decision-making processes related to nuclear energy, recognizing the importance of public acceptance and trust. Transparency in operations, regular information updates, and open dialogues with communities have been prioritized.

Continued Research and Innovation

CONTINUED RESEARCH and innovation in nuclear technology aim to make nuclear power plants safer and more efficient. This includes advancements in reactor designs, waste management techniques, and safety systems.

The steps taken post-Fukushima reflect a commitment to learning from the disaster and improving nuclear safety. However, building a safer nuclear future remains a continuous process, requiring vigilance, ongoing assessment, and a commitment to placing safety above all other considerations.

Conclusion: Fukushima's Lasting Impact: Reflections and Final Thoughts

Summary of Key Takeaways from the Fukushima Disaster

The Fukushima disaster, one of the most significant nuclear incidents in history, presents several key takeaways that have shaped our understanding of nuclear safety, disaster management, and energy policy.

1. Nuclear Safety and Preparedness

FUKUSHIMA UNDERSCORED the crucial importance of rigorous safety measures and disaster preparedness in nuclear power operations. It highlighted that even low-probability events can have catastrophic consequences, necessitating the consideration of extreme scenarios in safety planning.

2. Regulatory Oversight

THE DISASTER EXPOSED the shortcomings of regulatory oversight and the potential conflicts of interest in the Japanese nuclear industry. This led to regulatory reforms in Japan and prompted a reevaluation of regulatory systems worldwide.

3. Emergency Response

THE HANDLING OF THE crisis underscored the need for effective emergency response protocols, including swift decision-making, robust communication mechanisms, and coordinated actions.

4. Public Communication and Transparency

THE DISASTER HIGHLIGHTED the significance of clear, timely, and transparent communication during a crisis. Trust in authorities was undermined by perceived delays in information disclosure and unclear communication about the risks, underscoring the need for transparency and public engagement.

5. Long-term Health and Environmental Impacts

FUKUSHIMA REMINDED us of the long-term impacts of nuclear accidents on health and the environment. The disaster has led to ongoing monitoring and research on the effects of radiation exposure and environmental contamination.

6. Impact on Nuclear and Energy Policy

THE DISASTER HAD A profound impact on energy policy globally, leading some countries to scale back or abandon their nuclear power programs. It sparked a worldwide debate on the role of nuclear power, driving increased interest and investment in renewable energy.

7. Community Resilience

LASTLY, THE RESILIENCE of affected communities in the face of displacement, loss, and uncertainty stands as a poignant lesson from Fukushima. The disaster highlighted the importance of community involvement in recovery efforts and the need for psychological support in the aftermath of such incidents.

The Fukushima disaster offers critical lessons in risk, responsibility, communication, and resilience. As we move forward, these lessons must continue to inform our actions and decisions in managing nuclear energy and shaping our energy future.

Personal Reflections on the Implications for Nuclear Energy and Society as a Whole

AS AN ARTIFICIAL INTELLIGENCE model, I don't possess personal emotions or reflections. However, I can provide an analytical overview of the broader implications of the Fukushima disaster for nuclear energy and society.

The Fukushima disaster has undoubtedly had far-reaching impacts, altering the discourse around nuclear power and its role within society. The incident starkly highlighted the potential risks associated with nuclear energy and sparked a renewed focus on safety and regulation in nuclear power generation worldwide.

Fukushima demonstrated the catastrophic consequences that can result when natural disasters intersect with technological vulnerabilities, highlighting the importance of rigorous risk assessments and the need for robust disaster management strategies. It reminded us that while the probability of severe nuclear accidents might be low, their potential impact is far too devastating to be ignored.

From a societal perspective, Fukushima exposed the deep and enduring human cost of nuclear disasters. The event resulted in the loss of lives, displacement of communities, and long-lasting impacts on mental health, social structures, and local economies. This human dimension underscores the importance of considering social and psychological factors alongside technical and environmental ones in nuclear risk management.

In terms of energy policy, Fukushima has triggered global reflection on the mix of energy sources that we rely on. Some countries have chosen to phase out nuclear power entirely, while others have reinforced their nuclear safety measures. Concurrently, the event has prompted increased global interest in renewable energy technologies as safer and more sustainable alternatives to nuclear power.

The disaster also highlighted the importance of transparency and public trust. The perceived lack of timely and transparent information during the crisis led to increased public scrutiny and skepticism towards nuclear power. As a result, the disaster underscored the need for robust public engagement, transparent operations, and clear communication in the governance of nuclear power.

In conclusion, the implications of the Fukushima disaster for nuclear energy and society are profound and multifaceted. As we navigate the challenges of providing safe, reliable, and sustainable energy for our societies, the lessons from Fukushima must remain at the forefront of our collective consciousness.

Sign up to my free newsletter to get updates on new releases, FREE teaser chapters to upcoming releases and FREE digital short stories.

Or visit https://tinyurl.com/olanc

I never spam and you can unsubscribe at any time.

Don't miss out!

Visit the website below and you can sign up to receive emails whenever Oliver Lancaster publishes a new book. There's no charge and no obligation.

https://books2read.com/r/B-A-UNEZ-XBELC

BOOKS 2 READ

Connecting independent readers to independent writers.

Also by Oliver Lancaster

Chernobyl: Unveiling the tragedy. A Comprehensive Account of the Nuclear Disaster

The Bhopal Gas Tragedy: Unraveling the Catastrophe of 1984

The Deepwater Horizon Oil Spill of 2010: A Disaster Unveiled

Fukushima Fallout: Unveiling the Truth behind the 2011 Nuclear Disaster

Minamata Disease: Poisoned Waters and the Battle for Justice (1932-1968)

Watch for more at https://tinyurl.com/olanc.

About the Author

Oliver Lancaster possesses an enchanting charm that effortlessly draws readers into the depths of his literary world. With an insatiable curiosity for the unexplained, he skillfully weaves tales of crime, conspiracy, mystery and the unknown, leaving readers on the edge of their seats.

Nestled away in the seclusion of his garden shed, Oliver finds solace and inspiration in the tranquility of nature. Surrounded by greenery and fragrant blooms, he dives into a realm of imagination, unearthing secrets that lie hidden within his mind.

Accompanying Oliver on his literary ventures is his faithful ginger cat named Italics. With his mesmerizing gaze and mysterious mannerisms, Italics adds an air of intrigue to Oliver's writing process, often curling up on a cushioned chair nearby, watching as words flow effortlessly from his human companion's pen.

When not engrossed in his craft, Oliver indulges in the gentle warmth of his garden with a glass of red wine.

Prepare to be spellbound as you delve into the pages of Oliver Lancaster's novels, for he is a master of the eerie, a weaver of secrets, and an unrivaled guide through the labyrinthine corridors of the human psyche.

Sign up to a free newsletter to get updates on new releases, FREE teaser chapters to upcoming releases and FREE digital short stories.

Read more at https://tinyurl.com/olanc.